So, You Want to Work on Wall Street?

So, You Want to Work on Wall Street?

A guide to Wall Street and how to
manage your career to succeed!

Bob Alexander

To order additional copies of this book, contact:
Xlibris Corporation
1-888-795-4274
www.Xlibris.com
Orders@Xlibris.com
68048

CONTENTS

INTRODUCTION

You and some buddies are sitting around your dorm room one night talking about what to do with your $200K degrees. One says, "I'm going to be a CPA" and another says, "I am going to work for my family". It suddenly dawns on you that you are going for a Business Degree and have told anyone and everyone that you are going to work on Wall Street. But do you really know what Wall Street is? You begin to ask yourself, "What am I going to do on Wall Street, exactly?"

Well, don't worry, because you are about to read a book that is going to help you answer that question. This book is not one of those "How to Invest in the Markets" or "Ultimate Leadership" books. No names besides my own will be disclosed. My guidance is based on my real life experience. There will be no bashing of companies or people. It is a simple guide to assist you in understanding what Wall Street really is: how the firms are setup and organized; what are the jobs, roles, responsibilities, business lines, product lines, client bases, pitfalls, politics and functional departments that are out there. I have specifically kept this at a general and high level. There is much more detail about firms, products and groups to learn, but my goal here was to provide a broad overview so you can have a general understanding of the big picture. I have based this on structures that large firms on Wall Street tend to adapt, but it is important to note that every firm can and is sometimes different and does not always deal in the broad categories I will outline. Some are specific to products or business lines.

This book will assist you in defining what you enjoy and then aligning that with specific areas of Wall Street that will make you happy and ultimately successful. It will help you in looking for jobs that leverage your strengths, while working to minimize your weaknesses. It will give you some insight into and advice on managing your career. In short, it provides the details you need to determine if Wall Street is indeed right for you. I have worked on Wall Street for more than 20 years, and I was and am successful at what I do. I make good money and am always learning. I remember when I first started, though. I was scared to death. I knew nothing about Wall Street except that my dad worked there and people could make very good money doing it. Yes, even in bad times! The dilemma I faced was that I had no idea what "IT" really was. In my college days, what they taught didn't prepare me for what the real world of Wall Street was all about. Sure, they provided tons of financial formulas and economic theories, but not one course I took explained to me how to manage politics or how to decide what job I was best for or even what the jobs were, for that matter! To this day I am amazed that for all the money you spend on degrees, there is no outline for the real world of Wall Street. Nothing to help you decide what is right for you. Nothing that details the skills required to be successful in one of the largest and most complex industries in the world.

Well, there is now!!

WHAT ARE THE BUSINESS LINES

There are essentially three main business lines that all products and client bases fall under. They are:

- **Retail** (sometimes referred to as Private Client or Wealth Management)
- **Capital Markets** (Sales, Trading and Banking)
- **Investment Management**

All three interact tremendously, though some would say there are little synergies. I would argue to the contrary, as you will see. Each of them is aligned by either clients or products. I am limiting this section to the main areas within these Business Lines that are directly tied to revenue production. The types of personalities that succeed at these roles are generally fast-paced, intelligent and product oriented. The stress levels can be high in any one of them, though there is more stress in certain roles and groups than in others.

Retail

Not to oversimplify it, but this is best summed up by saying it is the supporting of the Toms, Charlies and Lisas of the world who want to invest money in the financial markets: individuals who want to buy or sell stocks and bonds or other financial instruments. They want to invest their money in products that will provide financial returns or preserve their investment.

The investors will interact with people called Retail Brokers. They go by many other names, such as Investment Advisers, Financial Consultants, Money Managers, Financial Advisors, Wealth Managers, Financial Planners, etc., etc. The list is virtually never-ending and there are a multitude of marketers employed on the street that keep coming up with more eye-popping titles every day. Call them what you want, but these people get paid to help individuals manage money and investments. They advise you on products that are available. They get paid commissions or fees on your trades or investment portfolio. The larger the trade or portfolio, the more they get paid, generally, usually regardless of whether you make or lose money.

The way it works is you will somehow get in touch with one of them. This is done by them calling you, being referred by a friend or you seeking them out yourself. They will sit with you to understand your financial situation—things like what you do for a living, what kind of income you have, what assets you possess, your age, when you want to retire, college funding, family financial needs, expenses, etc. It's an entire review specific to you and your needs financially. You will then open an account with them and deposit money or securities. They will then invest that money for you based on your needs and direction or at their discretion, if you have provided them authority to do so.

With the ongoing development of technology and access via online and discount brokers now available for individuals to invest on their own, Retail Brokers have had to adapt. Now most firms will allow you to open an account without having an advisor and let you invest on your own. On every trade, the firm will charge you a commission fee for executing your trades. They generally range anywhere from as low as $5 to hundreds of dollars, depending on the size of the trade. Investment firms have gotten savvy in expense management and have come to realize that the most profitable accounts are obviously the larger ones, and the smaller ones tend to cost them more money to support. Why should they have a high-priced adviser talking with a person about a $500 trade when that time can be spent on a millionaire? Some firms will not allow you to talk with an adviser unless you have a certain amount of assets, say $100,000, or unless you are willing to pay a minimal fee for the service. They will offer investors options on types of accounts that are better suited for the individual's needs, such as unlimited trading for a flat fee, or charge you a percentage on the amount of assets you hold with them. Fee structures are diverse and sometimes very complicated. Always read the fine print and understand what you are entering into and what you are subject to.

Retail itself has become more diverse, as well, and has expanded from the days of servicing Main Street into more complex products and structures. These days they will cater to small businesses or institutions to assist them in managing their assets. This is sometimes referred to as Middle or Small Capital Markets. These are firms that are generally too small to deal directly with a large Wall Street Trading and Sales desk, though from a support perspective, they are generally handled the same as Large Capital firms. In fact, even High Net Worth individuals are starting to get into more complex products such as derivatives and structured deals. The financial world is becoming an ever-increasingly complex arena and is constantly changing, and investors are adapting to it. In recent years, Retail has truly begun to merge with similar Banking activity. Once Glass Steagall (a law segregating certain banking, Insurance and brokerage businesses from one another) was repealed, it allowed banking and brokerage activities to integrate. Nowadays, you can go to the same person to get a mortgage, life insurance, retirement, checking, savings and an entire suite of other products. One-stop shopping has definitely hit Wall Street over the years, though in the current environment, who knows, maybe these laws will be reestablished. The important thing to note here is that Retail Brokers coordinate financial options for investors and bring a multitude of things together for them.

Retail has become more specialized. Just like anything, evolution is inevitable. On Wall Street, new products and ideas are a constant. There are now investment teams that will manage your assets. They can provide Tax advice and have a never ending offering of services they can provide, of course, for a fee. There are specialized areas to manage retirement plans for individuals and companies, as well as Topics such as Estate planning teams, Life and other Insurance coverage and College savings plans. Compare this to thirty years ago, when most people still only had savings accounts or a basic checking account. Now you can do everything in one place and if you have enough money, you can have your own financial team at your feet begging to service you and your assets.

It is important to note that in the retail space, no trading inventory is maintained. This is pure client servicing. They will facilitate your transactions and, more often than not, offer you a custodial arrangement for your assets. This is where the firm will hold the asset for the client. This is commonly referred to as *Hold* or *Custody* business. In certain cases, your assets can be held elsewhere and managed by a different firm. Most firms would prefer to hold them for you, as a key metric in this space is amount of assets they manage, and the more they hold the more they can charge and market. The assets are safeguarded by various industry laws, such as FDIC insurance or SEC 17A and 15C3, which means the firm cannot use an investor's assets without their permission and must ensure the assets are *locked up* and *secured*. They must attest to this on a regular basis via audits.

Capital Markets

This is really the core of the industry. The trades are big, the clients have massive amounts of assets, the products are diverse and complex and the cash flows are large. The clients are the biggest in the Financial World. Most major trading shops won't talk directly to investors unless they have at least $50 Million in capital. This is also sometimes referred to as Institutional Business, as it is very rare a Capital Markets desk will deal directly with an Individual Investor, though wealthy individuals are requesting this more and more. This is where the really big deals get done. At a high level, there are essentially two key areas that almost everything falls under in Capital Markets. They are Trading and Sales or Investment Banking. In the next chapter, we will explore the underlying groups and products. Research, as you will see, also generates revenue, as does other types of trading and services, but again, I am keeping this basic and general and as such will focus on the two main areas. We will touch briefly on other revenue generation areas later on.

Let's start with Trading, where the action happens. Wall Street Trading desks are some of the most exciting places in the world, but can also be some of the scariest. Traders take and initiate orders for the firm they work for or for the clients they cover. Some maintain inventory positions for things like Market Making (standing by to fill orders for a variety of reasons) or simply because they believe the position will make money. They are for the most part aligned to specific products.

The important thing here is that the Traders are the ones who buy and sell products for either the firm or clients. They are the ones facing exchanges or other counterparties. If a product is traded over an exchange, say the New York Stock Exchange (NYSE), the position is called Listed. The market transactions drive the pricing of these products. If the Product does not trade on an exchange, it is said to be OTC (Over the Counter) and trades are executed directly with counterparties at negotiated levels. As a general guideline, most Equity products are listed where a majority of Fixed Income products and Derivatives tend to be OTC. The pricing of these products is negotiable but Traders typically know what price range other traders are dealing these products in. There are different types of traders. The two most common are known as Proprietary and Agency.

Proprietary traders use the firm's capital to trade and make money for the firm. They put the firm's money to work. As a result of this, they are creating inventory for the firm. These positions are taken in to what is known as a Traders Book. Some books are shared by multiple traders while others are used by one trader only. There is obviously risk in this type of trading. The Traders are betting that markets will go a certain way. So if a trader shorts a position (sells it without owning it already), they are betting the market will go down so they can buy it at a lower price than they sold it. If they are long on a position, they are betting the market will go up. There are all different types of trades and products, some of which will be discussed later.

Agency Traders are known as risk-less Traders. This is because they typically will not hold positions in inventory. They will match orders. If a client wants to buy a certain product, these Traders will buy it from the market then sell it to the client. The Trader is flat or has no position at the end of the transaction and hence no risk.

Traders get paid off what Profit and Loss (P&L) they make for the firm. There are various means of tracking this P and L. Some are via realized (has happened) or unrealized (will happen) gains or losses, Mark to Market (re-pricing assets held) of the positions and a whole bunch of other things that come in to play, like cost of Funds (firms will charge Traders books for using the firm's capital). We will discuss the areas responsible for this later. A Proprietary Trader generates revenue, for one of many examples, by buying a product low and selling it high. An Agency trader makes Profit by what is called a spread or a mark up. For example, they will buy an asset and sell it at a higher price or with added fees to a client. In today's electronic world, firms are generating profit more so by fees than by markups.

A Trader's client base includes Sales, Retail Brokers, and other Traders on the street (also known as Broker to Broker Trades). There is another type of trader who sits on the floors of the exchanges. They are referred to as floor brokers or specialists. They work orders from clients and firms on the actual exchanges themselves and help maintain an orderly market.

Sales in Capital Markets are similar to Retail Brokers in a sense. They are both selling items, but that is pretty much where the comparison ends. Where Retail generally deals with individual investors, Capital Markets deals with Institutional investors. This includes but is not limited to Insurance companies, Pension Funds, Universities, Investment Managers, Hedge Funds, Corporate and Government Treasury departments and any other type of large Capitalized organization you can think of. Capital Market Sales people generally do not get paid by commissions. They are either compensated as a fee on a trade, paid not by the client but by the trading desks themselves or the business they facilitate for. This is tracked through what is called soft dollars. This is nothing more than a means of tracking how much business sales has generated for a Trader or a business.

Sales works in conjunction with Traders. Sales does not maintain inventory. They interact with Trading to facilitate trades or pricing of such for their clients. They are essentially middlemen for Trading and the clients. They have no P&L and, in a very real sense, are an expense that Trading is willing to pay from their P&L to generate more business.

Like Traders, there are all different types of sales people. Some work in teams, some are Relationship Managers, but a majority are aligned to a specific product line or even a client base. It all depends on the structure utilized within each firm. Investment Banking is really a mix between Trading and Sales, though probably aligned more to sales. Investment Banking is more of an advisory service. They deal with the senior executives of the corporate world and advise them about managing and raising capital. All of this is done for very large fees. The individuals who work in these groups are commonly known as Investment Bankers, and they have been the impetus behind some of the largest financial deals ever made on Wall Street.

Just like individuals, Corporations have money they need to put to work and they also need to raise capital for various reasons at any given moment in time. Investment Bankers will showcase new investment opportunities, advise on Mergers and Acquisitions, assist in firm financing and consult a takeover candidate on other options available—general overall management of a company's Capital. Investment Bankers interact with the utmost senior people of any Corporation, the Chief Executive Officers (CEO, CFO, COO), Board members and of course, Treasurers.

The average person associates Investment Bankers with the term Mergers and Acquisition (M&A), but this is not all they do. Of course they handle M&A, but they also bring new products to market, known as New Issuance. If a Corporation needs to raise capital, there are many ways to do that. You could sell assets, you could borrow or you could issue Bonds or Stock. Investment Bankers advise Corporations on all of this. Think of them as Investment Advisors for Corporations.

An example would better illustrate this. Let's say Company X is interested in buying Company Y. Both Companies might hire Investment Bankers to advise them, X on how best to approach the deal, how to raise capital needed, or the means on how X could purchase Y, be it through cash, stock or other means. They will advise Y on whether they should accept the offer or seek other means to stave off the offer. If Y is unwilling to be taken over, X is said to be making a hostile takeover bid. Investment Bankers, with a litany of lawyers at their side, handle all of this. If Stocks or Bonds are needed, they will handle the New Issuance to the marketplace as well. In the pecking order of prestigious roles on Wall Street, Investment Bankers have long been considered the top of the food chain.

Investment Management

This is also referred to as the *Buy Side*. Why you ask? Very simple: they buy assets from Capital market Trading desks (sometimes referred to as the *Sell Side*) that make up other products they then sell to clients. The Investment Management community consists of Traders, Portfolio Managers and Sales.

The term Investment Management is very appropriate for this part of the Financial Industry, as they manage investments for others. It is similar to Proprietary trading, but for client purposes rather than the Investment Management firm itself. They make money based on fees and commissions, fees because they will charge a fee for managingyour money or even for buying into one of the products they sell. They also sometimes charge commissions to buy and sell their products.

Traders at an Investment Manager are similar to Agency traders in Capital Markets. They will take orders from Portfolio Managers and usually place the orders with a Capital Markets desk, though in this day and age, some are going directly to exchanges for execution on listed products. They do not maintain inventory like Proprietary traders do. They are more so facilitators for those that are managing the actual products that are sold to the respective clients. Traders get paid on fixed scales generally, unlike Capital Markets Traders, who get paid on P&L as discussed.

Portfolio managers are the nucleus of the Investment Management world. They are managing pools of money and assets for clients and buying a variety of products to do so. They will place their orders through the trader, who will get them executed with a Capital Markets desk or an exchange directly as mentioned. Portfolio Managers are sometimes given a list of products that are suitable to purchase from the Chief Investment Officer. Others are given autonomy to invest funds as they see fit, assuming it fits into the investment objectives of the product or client they are investing for. One of the better known products an Investment Manager sells is called a Mutual Fund. I will explain more on this product later, but suffice it to say right now that it is a consolidation of investments into one product. So one Mutual Fund might have an objective of producing a return based on a specific index or exchange. The Portfolio Managers will choose which assets and in what percentages to purchase the assets within that index or exchange to produce the most optimal return. This is why so many similar funds actually produce different returns on investments. These are then consolidated into one product, a Fund. There are all different types of Portfolios, so obviously there are different types of Portfolio managers. They all generally do the same thing, though: invest pools of capital within a defined investment objective to produce the most optimal return for investors. Portfolio Managers are paid on the return they produce.

Sales people in Investment Management are similar as well to those in Capital Markets. They maintain relationships with Investors and Investor representatives such as Retail Brokers. They assist in creating new products to sell based on investor needs. Sales generally gets paid in a few different ways. They can be paid on a flat scale, as a percentage on the assets they bring in to be managed or based on return they generate for clients.

How They Interact

Though many would think these are all segregated and detached from each other, they interact on a regular basis. If you recall, I stated that Capital Market Traders maintain Inventory, while Retail Brokers and Investment Managers do not. They custody and manage assets for clients and/or for the Investments they create for clients. Hence Retail Brokers and Investment Managers are clients of Capital Market Trading. In fact, many Capital Market Trading desks have segregated areas to support these order flows. The primary point here is that Investment Managers and Retail Brokers will go to Capital Markets for products, as they are the ones that house or have the relationships with the street or exchanges. This is certainly not the only extent to which they interact. At many firms in which all three business lines coexist, similar functions and roles are leveraged, as well as technology in certain cases. Having said that, every firm I know who has all three business lines needs to do much more leveraging to reduce expenses—just a personal observation from my experience.

Because Investment Mangers and Retail Brokers are clients of Capital Markets, the service that is provided by the areas supporting Capital Markets is highly linked with Investment Management and Retail Brokerage. As a result of the execution linkage, the servicing of all three is all highly related.

Most of the firms that have all three are extremely large and create their own walls and silos. One of my favorite sayings about these firms is that someday they will get out of their own way and make a boat-load of money. There is much waste in expenses and if one can look across a firm and streamline similar activities, expenses would go down and hence profitability up. In these days, where revenues are drying up quickly, and margins are tightening, expenses are even more heavily scrutinized. Consolidating is not an easy fix, as most things on Wall Street are not easy fixes, but I truly believe the best and brightest firms that will survive in the long run have no choice but to reengineer and leverage similar functions. I also believe the days of reengineering in general have come though some firms are short-sighted and not willing to spend money to save money in the long run. Volume and complexity is through the roof, with record levels across the board. Today's processes and technology cannot support them in a controlled manner. The trick is to be able to handle the current complexity and volumes with room for expansion in a cheaper and more efficient manner, while improving time to market and the service you are providing your clients. The people and firms that will excel at this are the ones with the broadest knowledge base, those who can see the big picture and deliver it.

Now for the personalities. Retail and Investment Managers for the most part are longer term investors and as such are not in as much of a hurry to show profit immediately. More so, they measure profitability over time, say a year or so. Capital Markets are for today. Hence the pace in Capital Markets tends to be much faster and more stressful than in Investment Management or Retail. Don't misunderstand me, please, they can all be stressful; I simply believe that the mentality and pace of the organization is more often than not directly aligned to its Investment objectives, and as such requires different approaches to work in them. I worked in all three at one point or another in my career and I can honestly say that Capital Markets was more energetic because it is at the center and the requirement there is to deliver today. One must be intelligent, diligent and hard working to succeed in any of them, though.

THE BASICS

Now that you have a general understanding of the revenue producing areas of Wall Street, let's turn our focus to how they are structured, what products are involved and what other areas are required for them to run effectively on a daily basis. Last but certainly not least, we will touch on the subject of service.

General Structure

The basic Wall Street organizational structure consists of revenue producers and support teams. The support areas are very broad and diverse. Not every support area is directly linked to a revenue group, as you will see. For the most part, all revenue areas are aligned with a product or client base. Retail is aligned predominantly for clients, though there are specific product areas as well, for topics such as Retirement accounts, Mortgages, etc., but from a large picture, Retail Brokers are client-centric. Capital Markets tend to be divided by products, Equity and Fixed Income. Traders will handle specific product lines, as will Sales, though some Sales teams are focused on clients broadly. Relationship Management teams would be a good example. Investment Banking is traditionally organized by industry category of the client: Insurance, Governments, Financials, etc. Investment Management is a mix of client and product aligned.

Support Divisions

There are many support divisions that have specific units dedicated to a business or product line, but there are also many that are somewhat generic and slice across all aspects of the organization. The following will list the support divisions and provide a brief description of what the responsibilities of that department are. This should provide insight to the type of personality required to work in any one of them. Many of these areas do have sub-groups which I will briefly touch on.

Human Resources

This department handles all of the employees and related issues. This is a department that does cut across an entire firm. They are neither product nor business specific, as every area has employees, obviously. They take care of orienting employees into the firm as well as the departure of employees due to termination, resignation or retirement. They maintain all the employee files and related data. They are responsible for coordinating the distribution and tracking of compensation and employee benefits. In addition, they organize all employee training as relating to development. Development does not include any regulatory licensing, though, as that is typically handled by compliance due to registration needs and the regulatory relationships. They also handle any internal jobs that are being offered as well as special needs employees might have such as career advice, trauma or stress from the job or related topics (9/11 as an example). Human Resources, like many groups, goes by many names. They can be called many different things like Employee Resources or Learning and Talent Management, etc. At the end of the day, they handle all the administrative needs surrounding employees. Typically each division or department within an organization will have a team or representative group dedicated to them and their staff. Human Resource staff tend to be very pleasant and conservative individuals. They are polished and professional. They need to be, as they are usually the first and last point of contact for employees or potential employees to deal with.

Treasury

Almost every firm has a Treasury Department, as every firm has money or assets that need to be managed or the need to raise capital. The staff here serves as a liaison with the various business units that invest or utilize capital and the other financing sources in the market. The Treasury Department configures the most productive way to get funding from sources to the businesses that require it. Some firms do not manage capital or the cost of raising such effectively. Many charge an average cost of raising money rather than directly charging the actual cost, and many charge legal entities rather than specific business units for the use of capital. Needless to say, this annoys Business Units, as they do not know the true cost of using capital to execute their business. Treasury is not necessarily meant to be a revenue producing unit, but does create profit or loss. At a very high level, they consolidate the firm's assets at the end of each day, week or some fixed period of time and determine the need to either invest or raise capital by either borrowing, lending or issuing debt or cash in one form or another. If a firm is a multiple currency organization, they are responsible for managing Foreign Exchange back to the source currency the company is base operating in. So, for example, a US-based company may deal in all parts of the world, but as it is based in the US, the US dollar is its primary currency and everything must get managed back to USD. They are the financing arm of the corporation. The individuals that tend to do well in this department have a firm grasp on managing finances. They are organized, understand various markets and how to invest and raise capital. As with all other support and revenue teams, they are professional. Treasury has many tentacles and does have other groups that support it on a daily basis. Some examples include Operations, Finance, Human Resources and Technology. They do tend to act and look like a Business Unit for the most part, but in my opinion, they are there to provide support for the revenue producers of the firm.

Executive Management

This group is pretty obvious. They are the leaders of the firm, the most senior people; the Chairman, Chief Financial Officer, Presidents, etc. They are accountable to the Board of Directors and the shareholders if it is a public company. They are the ones that set the direction of the firm and make the real big and tough decisions. They set the strategy or direction of the firm and ultimately define where or where not to invest or build. Now, having said that, I have found in my interactions that they tend to be extremely intelligent and smart individuals. Some can lose a feel for the organization at times, which is a very dangerous place to be. This is not the case for all, mind you, as I have seen some that are very in tune with the lowest levels of an organization! They have a real feel for the organization and are very involved in the daily businesses. If you are fortunate enough to work under executives that are like this, consider yourself very lucky. Again, this is not to say they are not highly intelligent and switched on. They are. You do not get to these levels without being such. These folks make large money for this, as well. Anyone who reads a firm's financials or the papers these days knows exactly what I am talking about. Millions!! They tend to be highly polished, political, very articulate and are extremely strategic and financially savvy.

Real Estate and Facilities Management

This is another area that can cut across the firm in its entirety. Every firm has office space and real estate it must manage. You would be surprised how much maintenance there is or how expensive these groups tend to be. Some of these groups are outsourced to management companies or even leveraged within Business Units that invest or manage Real Estate. Regardless, they are there and they are an essential part of any organization. They handle everything from changing light bulbs, installing carpet, building cubicles, hanging pictures and custodial duties to managing space, vendor management, cafeterias and floor build outs. This is a pretty diversified group, actually, as it consists of management professionals through to contractors. Enough said, really.

Technology

This is one of the most dynamic and ever-changing areas of any organization. It touches every group in one way or another. I can recall when I started on Wall Street in the 1980s, when these groups were very small. We didn't have emails or Instant Messaging. We had wire systems and operators. More often, records were physically maintained. If you go even further back, they had nothing but physical paper. Technology has contributed by far the most to the expansion on Wall Street in every form imaginable, be it Trading platforms, electronic communications, desktops, etc. The introduction of technology to the business world was like an explosion. It afforded the opportunity for never before seen growth and product expansion. It has improved productivity and efficiency. One could say an enabler obviously and to a certain extent allowed Wall Street to get ahead of itself. As products got more complex and people began to rely on technology to manage risk and products, it has greatly removed the people aspect from the business and subsequently gotten ahead of itself. These days, technology from even a year ago could be outdated. It is a never-ending cycle of growth and expansion. People rely on emails rather than phone calls. I have absorbed more losses as a result of technology and people not following through than I care to remember. Technology is a fabulous tool, but don't ever forget that people build technology and not the other way around, for the time being, anyway. In my view, technology could never replace the strength of a person to person relationship. Don't ever forget that.

Now back to the group itself. As I mentioned, it is broad and deep. There are all different types of technology teams across Wall Street. Most people think this group is a bunch of programming technologists. On the contrary, these are some of the brightest and best leaders I have had the privilege to work with. The best technologists that I have encountered are not just smart about technology. They know the business. These are not programmers who sit in a back room just typing away, writing code. They are engaged and at the forefront of changing and driving the business forward. Take electronic trading. Who would have thought 20 years ago that any individual could sit on their couch and execute a trade? And what about instantly speaking face to face with someone on the other side of the world? No, these are innovators and pioneers. Sure, there are the programming types, but there is so much more than that in this space.

There are programmers, developers, project managers, vendor managers, administrative managers and more. I have run across Chief Technology Officers that have never written code a day in their lives, though as with everything else, they do tend to rise from the bottom and more often than not are historic code writers. This organization also is cross organizational, but does have business specific lines. This, too, is an area that should be leveraged more and more across a firm to reduce cost. As a point of information, most firms have their largest cost allocations through technology. The sad thing is that most are allocating a majority to maintenance rather than development. I remember an executive mentor of mine once telling me that a growth and futuristic company should be spending 10-15% of its technology budget on maintenance and the rest on development. I believe this to be true. There is a tremendous opportunity for consolidation in this space on Wall Street. Watch this space, as you have an area that is the driving force behind change and innovation, yet the biggest expense line in your budgets and sometimes not very well leveraged. Most firms have too much technology. This has to change, and real soon, in my opinion.

Firm technology teams are traditionally broken into a few groups. There are the programmers and developers that write code and work on enhancing existing or delivering new technologies. Then there are the desktop support teams. These are areas that help every employee with daily problems they are experiencing on the computers they have on their desks. There are business technologists that sit within business units delivering technology specific to products or clients, enhancing the client experience or providing better service levels—electronic client statements, for example. There are strategy teams to figure out how technology can be best leveraged across the firm with the idea of quick and efficient data access. Speed is essential in today's world of technology. There are application support teams that solely work on maintaining or enhancing existing platforms that are in use today. Then, of course, there is the management above these groups. The types that excel in this area are creative, innovative and personable. Yes, believe it or not, personable. There is a tremendous amount of people interaction within technology. You have to if you are going to deliver good products or services to your clients. As mentioned, they tend to rise from coding and grow through the ranks. This is a space that will never go away. It has changed the world around us and will continue to—not a bad place to be, if you ask me.

Operations

I have worked in Operations for more than 23 years. I did so consciously, as well. There was logic to my madness. I was fortunate enough at a very young age to know that I enjoyed problem solving. I was also fortunate enough to have been provided exposure to Wall Street. When I began, I immediately started thinking about where is the center of all the problems. I found Operations. Many people look at the term operations and think of building or processing. They are correct. For my money, barring technology, there is not any other area on Wall Street that affords one the opportunity to interact with every area of a firm's business or, for the aggressive individual, to learn the most about it. Operations are the center of processing. Yes, technology enables and cuts across all, but Operations processes all. Almost every other group is reliant on Operations to get their jobs done correctly. Operations controls all the cash and security movements, entries to customer accounts, reconciliations, processing of Trading inventories, setup and maintenance of data, client confirmations and statements and call centers, to just name a few. Operations are the servicing engine of the organization and Wall Street.

There are areas of operations that are firm-wide and other parts that are product or business unit aligned. There are typically areas with sub-groups beneath them. One example that traditionally will support all areas is referred to as Asset Servicing. This group consists of the following components:

- Corporate Actions/Reorganization—They process dividends, Interest Coupons and asset changes that are on the books of the firm.
- Cash and Security settlements—They process and move the cash and securities in and out of the firm.
- Reference Data—They process and maintain data as relates to Product and Client information, like security descriptions and related information, as well as any and all detail that relates to a client, such as name and address, cash and security settlement instructions, to just name a few.

Then there are areas that are product or business line specific:

- Client Services—This is a generic term, as all the Business Lines do have different Client types and as such each client type has different needs. So for example, in Retail or Investment Management, there might be call centers with technology that can handle client requests, as many are repetitive inquiries, whereas in capital markets clients prefer to speak with a someone immediately and have the problem resolved ASAP and not have to go through a machine. This area services clients.
- Business support staff—In capital Markets this would be Trading and sales desk support, segregated by specific products such as Municipal Bonds or Equity Portfolio Trading. They are processing trades, confirming orders with clients and pretty much anything else a Trader or Sales person asks them to do. In Retail, this would be Financial Advisor assistants. They deal directly with client queries of a specific FA, process orders for the FAs, obtain client information and again pretty much anything the FA might need done.

- Then there are very specific product support groups. An example would be Collateral Management. This is a group that manages collateral as it relates to products traded with clients in which the firm requires collateral to be posted against the deal to minimize exposure on such. This group should be aligned very closely with Credit, as will be obvious to you shortly. A similar group in retail is the Margin department. The difference between these groups is really the rules and guidelines they follow. Collateral is very deal and client specific, where margin guidelines are standard formulas driven by regulators and internal compliance areas per product. Both seek to minimize exposure to the firm but have some assets to cover market exposure.
- Retail will have a dedicated team to specific products, as well. Examples would include Retirement or College savings accounts. There are specific processing needs for these areas as opposed to, say, Statement Quality Assurance which validates and ensures the accuracy of a client statement.
- Operational Control is another area that most business units or even functional groups all have respectively. These are the teams that reconcile everything. They monitor and measure risk and exposure to specific areas, products or functions. This is where I started and really began to learn the business. I always tell people this is a tedious and mundane role but, if done right, it can teach you much. It affords two basic concepts. First, if you are reconciling a business or process, you should know that business or process as well as, if not better, than the ones doing it. It is a learning opportunity, to say the least. Second, and probably even more valuable, it teaches a very difficult skill set under the topic of communications. Communications is a huge area, and I could probably write a book on that topic alone. Think about it this way in Control, though. You are identifying problems that have occurred. You are then telling the individual that made the mistake that they did so and that you want to help get it resolved. Most people do not want to hear that they made a mistake much less that the person who found it wants to help them. Master that and it will benefit you beyond work, I assure you.

These are but a few of the areas of Operations. There are many, many more that are product specific, given that each product has its own nuances. There are even revenue producing areas within Operations. Examples include Custody and Clearance. Service has become a commodity and many organizations will sell that service to others.

Operations is a great place to learn for the individual who has the right drive and desire to do so. One must be process and service oriented, diligent in that process and able to deal with multiple types of individuals and personalities. Historically, the folks in this area were the blue collar workers on Wall Street. Today they are viewed more as business partners.

Credit

This is an absolutely vital role in the firm that, in my opinion, needs broader focus from management and regulators in general. If this department makes mistakes, it could cost a firm dearly. This area is responsible for monitoring the risk and exposure associated with specific clients, a client base or even products that corporations issue, as corporations are clients. This department is heavily integrated with Trading and Sales as well as the Client Data groups of a firm. The types that are successful in this area are risk focused, analytical, street savvy of names of institutions and their relationships and are in tune with the overall markets in general.

Risk

This area is similar to Credit; however, they monitor the risk of products a firm holds in Trading Inventories. These are typically the so called *Quant's* of the world. They set and monitor inventory risk levels by products rather than by clients. This is also extremely important, as if a firm takes on too much risk in any particular product, they can get in a lot of trouble. Just look at what happened in the Asset Backed Securities space recently for Mortgage products. This group is also responsible to ensure that Inventory is properly hedged to ensure that any potential losses are minimized. Bad hedging can bring a firm to its knees very quickly. These people keep the Traders on the straight and narrow. You can probably see by now that Wall Street is very much about checks and balances. This group is one of the most critical, as it keeps firms in check on the amount of risk they take. The ones that succeed in this group are extremely sharp with regard to analytics, product knowledge, market information and mathematics. These people really should be smarter than the traders they are supporting when it comes to understanding the products that are being traded.

Audit

More checks and balances. There are usually internal and external audit teams. The external audit team is typically an accounting firm that is responsible for regulatory sign-off and scrutiny, as well as ensuring the accuracy of a firm's financial statements. The internal team is somewhat of a precursor to them. They are the ones that go around the firm and ensure best procedures and practices are in place and are being adhered to so the external audits can go smoothly. This relates to every aspect of the firm. This group will assign teams to go into a department and scrutinize how things are processed, maintained and controlled and then make recommendations on how it can be done better, particularly to be in line with industry and regulatory standards. The group typically is made up of accountants, though, as Audit typically falls under an Accounting structure. Some firms are beginning to switch to employing a more diversified skill set in Audits, placing experts from various other aspects and functions of an organization that can hit the ground running and are familiar with specific processes, functions and products.

The types that excel here are focused on risk mitigations. They are very diligent and analytical when it comes to reviewing flows and procedures. Accountants are good for the financials as mentioned, as they crunch the numbers. Broad knowledge of Wall Street is a plus, particularly on what areas do, why they do it, regulatory rules and the best practices to accomplish this. As with any and all groups, strong communication skills are a must.

Finance

These people are unfairly known as the bean counters, though they do so much more than track the numbers. They are vital partners for the Business Lines and, like other areas, must be attached at the hip with many support groups. There are many different areas within this organization. There are Business Unit Finance, Corporate Finance, Regulatory Control, Project Management teams, and then there is what I like to call Support Finance.

Business Unit Finance are teams dedicated to the business lines, so Retail has a dedicated team to track and post profit and losses of Financial Advisors. Capital Markets has similar, usually broken down into Equity, Fixed Income and Investment Banking units. At a high level, these folks track the Profit and Losses daily of the revenue producers in their respective organizations, both realized and unrealized, and ensure that the entries are properly posted in the Financial ledgers of the firm. They also handle things like ensuring Traders mark books correctly for positions they own, validating them to the street quotes, as well as ensuring proper compliance within accounting standards.

Corporate finance does similar. They roll up the Profit and Loss of all groups to the Corporate or Parent level. However, this group typically has some broader groups and responsibilities. Other groups that usually are encompassed under Corporate Finance include Regulatory Reporting, Accounting Policy and Treasury Finance. Regulatory Reporting is responsible for filing financials with regulators and ensuring adherence to all related rules, such as maintaining proper liquidity levels or available capital. Accounting Policy is responsible for opining on accounting policy that all areas of Finance must comply with. This would include things like New product P&L or accepting new accounting standards such as Fair value accounting etc. Treasury Finance is like BU Finance in that it tracks the financials for the Treasury group. Treasury is constantly borrowing and lending money and this is tracked typically by Finance.

Then there is Support Finance—not much to this, really. They track the financials for all the support groups. Usually each Support group has its own dedicated team. They, like the other Finance Units, monitor expenses. But support groups do not generate P&L. They are usually expenses only, unlike the Business lines that have P&L and expenses. The expenses that support generates are mapped back to Business Lines in some shape or form. Support Finance monitors these expenses and works with the respective Support divisions as well as the receiving business centers that are taking the expenses.

Needless to say, the types that are successful here are very good with numbers and spreadsheets. Interpersonal skills are a plus, and product and business knowledge goes a long way.

Legal and Compliance

This area consists of the lawyers as well as the Compliance officers of the firm. Like other support groups, they are broken down to support various areas of a firm. On the lawyer front, there are business lawyers who advise on deals, new issuances, mergers and other legalities associated with investments. Then there are litigation lawyers that deal with lawsuits the firm is involved in. There are also lawyers to advise on situations such as decisions that have potential legal implications. This would include things such as amending verbiage on statements or letters that need to be sent to clients. Corporate Law is big business and there tend to be some very bright people in this area.

Compliance is the area that tracks and ensures that the firm is acting in compliance with all the rules it is obligated to as a Financial Services firm. This is different from Regulatory in that Compliance tends to track more specific things such as trading activity, employee licensing or any rules the firm must comply with dependent on how it is set up in the financial sector, i.e., as Broker Dealer or as an Investment Manager, etc. For example, if an Investment Manager has issued Mutual funds and they are SEC 40 Act funds, there are rules and regulations that must be met and adhered to so they can state they are a 40 Act fund. Compliance ensures these criteria are met and maintained. This is a very important aspect to the business, as non-compliance gets your name in the newspapers or fined, and no firm wants bad publicity or fines.

The types that are found here are pretty conservative. Obviously, lawyers are lawyers and I need not mention them. But Compliance officers tend to be very book-smart folk. They understand rules and regulations, similar to lawyers understanding the laws. They generally tend not to be the most outgoing of individuals, nor are they necessarily product-savvy. There are exceptions, of course. Both know the rules and laws and what needs to be done to comply with such.

Marketing and Research

Some would say these actually fall under Business Lines. I am not of that opinion. These areas are vital to the Business Lines and more so to clients, but for the most part do not produce revenue, though firms do sometimes charge a fee for the Product and Industry Research they provide. Usually that fee is incorporated into what the Business Lines are charging clients for doing business with them. There are times where they simply charge for research access, though. Marketing, on the other hand, is generally an expense to the firm. One could argue that by marketing you are attracting more business, hence my point that they could be associated under revenue production.

Research could not be named more appropriately. This group consists of economic, product and industry experts that analyze anything and everything that can affect the products or markets they are covering. They then provide opinions on what they believe is occurring and could occur based on the facts they have reviewed. For industries, they will give an overview of the industry and what is currently going on and then look at external factors such as employment data, interest rates or Foreign exchange rates and make judgments on how those external factors will affect the industry. They will also provide advice on economics globally and within each country. The world has become a very consolidated place so economies, industries and products are very much intertwined. The old saying, one country sneezes and another catches a cold is true. For products, it is much the same. For Equities or Corporate bonds, they will analyze the companies themselves. They do this by looking at revenue trends, Financial Statements, pipeline business, available cash, rating agency data, etc., and then making recommendations on whether to buy, sell or hold the asset. Each firm has its own type of rating system so I will spare you the details. Needless to say, though, the statements that these people make affect the value of the products and firms. If a top known research analyst comes out and states the equity is a sell, it's a pretty good bet that stock will drop in value, and if a few of them do it, the odds are even better.

Marketing is more or less advertising, getting your name out there and letting the public know about what you do or what products or services you have to offer. Most major firms, not only on Wall Street, spend fortunes on this stuff. They do this in a variety of formats, big and small. It could be sponsoring Golf events, buying advertising time during the Super Bowl, signs on the highway, newspaper or magazine ads, etc. The list is virtually endless. They also do it via mailings, flyers, seminars and emails, to name some of the smaller ones.

The individuals that work in these groups are very different. Research people are very analytical and street savvy. They understand economics, financial statements and products, whereas Marketing are more advertising types. They are analytical, but are selling the corporate name and the products of such, outgoing and friendly people that are very cognizant on how to reach markets and individuals.

Business Administration

This is a generic unit that almost every group, be it revenue producing or support, generally has. Yes, it includes the executive assistants or what used to be referred to as secretaries that handle the administrative aspects of answering phones, setting up meetings, ordering food, paying department bills and handling all the employee requests such as travel, expense reporting or ordering supplies. But there is a broader role within this topic. Somewhat of a jack of all trades, in some groups they are called Business Managers or Chief Operating Officers, but whatever the term used, they are coordinators in truth. On the business side, they tend to be known as Chief Operating Officers. They are the ones that track revenue and expenses and work with various support groups on ensuring the business lines are getting properly supported. They are also the ones that handle the administrative aspects of getting new products approved. They are usually not revenue producers themselves, but are critical to ensuring preservation of such as well as working to reduce expenses that get charged to business lines. They also are the lead drivers of any initiatives such as technology builds or enhancements that the business lines require to be more successful and efficient. They have good knowledge of the specific business lines they support, as well as a broad understanding of the impacts other areas have on such. On the support side, it is similar, but tends to be more of a Project Management role. They will work with multiple areas to ensure proper reporting and expense management, but they will also coordinate the initiatives that your typical project managers are not handling. I was always a big fan of people like this because as a senior manager, it is virtually impossible to do everything yourself and you need a solid coordinator to drive things for you. I would use them for employee training, expense management, project initiatives and a multitude of fire drills that would come across my desk on a daily basis. These people tend to be very organized, possess a broad array of knowledge of the organizations and are results-oriented. Again, solid communication skills are a must.

Service Structure

Every firm structures the alignment of groups differently. For example, in certain firms the front office support of Operations is combined with the Finance teams, the logic being that there are synergies between getting trades booked correctly and timely, with the reporting of P&L, amongst other things. Then there are examples where Operations is actually within the Business Lines. The Prime Brokerage business is a great example, as at its core, prime Brokerage is really selling Operational services, predominantly clearance. However it is aligned, there are a few structures that should always be adhered to from a control perspective alone. Risk and Credit should never fall within the Business Lines, as there could be a conflict of interest. These groups are meant to police the business, if you will, and should not be managed by the very groups they are monitoring. Usually audit will restrict certain structures. Any way you look at it, there are two primary groups, regardless of reporting lines: those that generate revenue and the groups that support the revenue producers. Then there are examples where Business Lines are imbedded within support. An example of this is revenue producing areas, such as custody, where firms charge fees for holding and reporting client assets. This could be and usually is incorporated under Operations. On the Retail side, many firms have placed limitations on who gets to talk with Financial Consultants. This is reserved for larger asset based accounts, say over $100K. The smaller accounts are pushed to service center models in which service consultants, usually under the Operations umbrella, present advice or consultation. There are valid arguments for various structures, but at the end of the day, all these groups must work together efficiently for any firm to be successful. All groups must strive to provide the best service and products to clients in an efficient and cost effective manner. Technology automation has greatly assisted this process, as these days you can handle much more volume of more complex products in a quicker and more efficient format.

As stated earlier, Service has become a commodity and as such, is vital to clients, revenue, expenses and risk mitigation. The firms that excel at providing the best service across these categories will, in my opinion, be the firms of tomorrow. The others will be overtaken or disappear.

Products

In an effort to not weigh you down too much on this, I will cover different types of accounts and products within each of the three core business lines. This is high level and if any of these products sparks a unique interest to you, I would highly recommend further research via the web, calling a Financial Consultant or even getting a book on a specific product. Believe me, there are loads out there. The Internet provides some very good insight for free. In addition, there are many financial formulas out there, which your professors beat into you, I'm sure, in class. The Internet does have very good sites to further explain them, as well. I am staying away from them, as that is not what this book is about, as you can see. The following account and product guideline does not cover every type out there. New products and accounts are created all the time. This is meant to give you a broad and general understanding of the major types that exist.

Retail is more driven by type of client and types of accounts, as the assets they require are sourced from Capital Markets or Investment Management, as previously discussed. There are all different types of accounts on Retail Wall Street. The more common types are really broken down in to a few basic categories which are Savings, Investment Speculation and Income.

Savings accounts are very broad. It all depends on what you are saving for. Some people might be saving for retirement, college, a house or just for asset preservation. Within each there are specific accounts with very different structures from the perspectives of tax implications, investment styles and even restrictions on what can and cannot be purchased. They all have their own rules and restrictions, ultimately to protect the clients. Retirement accounts come in many forms. There are 401K plans that large corporations create for employees; there are various Individual Retirement Accounts (IRAs) such as Sep IRAs and KEOGHs that small business owners set up for employees; there are Pension Plans in which companies will pay employees even after they retire. The common goal is that these are focused on creating availability of funds for when you are not working anymore. College Savings really came on the scene some years ago, given the soaring cost of extended education and the easing of tax requirements over the years on these types of accounts. The most common is known as 529 Plans. This allows individuals to put away a certain amount of money and invest it with the intention of using it for college expenses later, usually with no tax event on the investment. Then there are just plain savings accounts in which people deposit money and get a return in the form of interest payments on a regular basis. Firms take these deposits and invest them in things like Money Markets, Certificates of Deposit, etc. The general premise is the firm will pay you but they are usually earning more than what they are paying you, hence generating revenue. This is heavily regulated these days due to bank failures over the years.

Investment Speculation is when individuals and small investors want to play the markets in the hope they can trade and make money. As they are typically not what are known as sophisticated investors, there are limitations placed on what they can and cannot purchase, though firms are becoming more and more creative in creating products which will get them the same exposure as investing in the restricted product. Derivative products are a great example. Most individuals are restricted from purchasing derivatives, so firms have created notes in which the underlying economics of the note is actually a derivative. The limitations are placed because of the risky nature of these products and they typically are not suitable for the average individual investor. These accounts are for clients that want to buy and sell stocks and bonds or even options or futures. They are betting the markets are going to go higher or lower, depending on what they have traded. More often than not, these accounts will be set up as Margin accounts, meaning clients can leverage the accounts based on the amount of assets they have in the account. This allows them to not pay the full amount on the investments and firms will charge Margin Interest on the extended balances. Put simply, firms will lend you money based on what assets you have with them.

The last type is Income. These are for the conservative types who have assets and want to preserve what they have while making some money at the same time. These are safer investment styles. Clients will buy assets that pay dividends or coupons or have these reinvested for growth purposes. This is probably where the phrase "you have to have money to make money" came from. The accounts in here are things like Trust and Estate accounts and not Margin—very similar to savings accounts. These accounts are very common with retired people who have assets and live within a fixed income structure.

Investment Management is a combination of Retail and Capital Markets, as they have direct clients but create products themselves. The most common product is known as a Mutual Fund, and there are all different types to expose investors to the gamut of investment opportunities that exist on Wall Street. Mutual Funds are when a Investment Manager takes clients' money and purchases many different types of assets, then consolidates and packages it up into one product called a Mutual Fund. An example is a High Yield fund, where the objective of the fund is to provide a High Yield return based on purchasing High Yielding assets such as bonds or equities. The performance of each underlying asset is tracked daily and consolidated in to what is called a Net Asset Value (NAV). This is the price or value of the fund itself. It is meant to give a broad range of investments rather than a single one to investors. They are considered safer than individual investments, as it hedges a portfolio by not being exposed to just one asset. Mutual funds are sold off directly to clients from the Investment Manager or through Financial Consultants. Other types of products are Separate Account Management and Alternative Investments. Separate Account Management is when investors hire an Investment Manager to invest money for them. They take money from clients and create specific portfolios, similar to a Mutual Fund, and charge a Management Fee to do so. The sell here is that a professional can manage your money better than you can. Alternative Investments is relatively new. As more sophisticated and complex products have been created, clients have a desire to invest in them. Again, Derivatives is the most common. Investment Managers will create funds that have Derivatives as the underlying assets.

The Capital Markets business line is predominantly divided by product classes. The most common type of account is Investment speculation, as very large investors are dealing with trading desks directly. Assets are typically bought and sold and then delivered or received from the client versus payment. This is also known as DVP/RVP, Deliver Versus Payment or Receive Versus Payment.

The two primary product classes of Capital Markets are Equity (Stocks) and Fixed Income (Bonds). Equity is more straightforward as a stock is a stock, whereas in Fixed Income they will further break it down into bonds that trade based on Credit or bonds that trade based on interest rates, Rates. I am also going to discuss one other, Prime Brokerage, as it generally slices across all products.

Equities can be summarized by stating it is stocks. Stock is a representation that the ownership of such constitutes an equity stake in the organization that has issued the stock.

There are all different types of stocks. I will cover the more common types. The Equities business for the most part consists of the following areas:

Portfolio Trading: This when multiple stocks are purchased and packaged into a portfolio for clients. The client will provide a list of stocks s/he wishes to purchase and the Trading Desk will purchase them and usually provide an overall price of the Portfolio itself for the client. Also referred to as Average Pricing. So if in the Portfolio the client asked one of the stocks to be X, and the amount was purchased in numerous orders, the overall price for obtaining X is provided on the average price of all the purchases. This has become most useful for firms when selling what is known as I shares, a conglomeration of stocks that is consolidated into one stock. This is similar to a Mutual fund but does not carry all the fees and costs associated with such.

Equity Derivatives and Financing: Also referred to as Equity Swaps, these are derivations of stocks. There are loads of different types that play off interest rates, indexes or stocks themselves. One side is betting one way on something and the counterparty another. So in the example of an Index Derivative, one side might pay a premium to bet the Index will move one way, while the other is betting it moves a different way. They are also seen as a way to finance your position, so one firm might own a certain stock and lend that stock for a fee to another. This is also known as Stock lending. The lending firm benefits by not having the asset on its books for a period and receives cash, while the other uses the stock it receives to settle a trade, for example, when it did not have the asset to settle. The side receiving the stock is known as the Borrower.

Convertible Bonds: These are Bonds, but they are usually aligned with equities, as they can be converted into the equity of the issuing company at a certain time.

Depository Receipts: There are American (ADR) and Global (GDR) Depository receipts. These are best described as financial securities that are listed on a local stock exchange but issued by a publicly listed foreign company.

Preferred Stock: It is another form of an Equity that typically carries more protection in the pecking order of payment if a company goes belly-up and has more voting rights than common equity stock holders.

Electronic Trading: This is also sometimes referred to as Program Trading or Direct Market Access. In short, it is direct execution of orders with exchanges electronically. It has revolutionized the way Equities trade forever and has afforded better order routing as well as better price execution levels for all involved.

New Issues: Also referred to as the Primary Market. This is an arm of Investment Banking. This is the group that coordinates bringing new equity to the market. It then will trade on what is known as the Secondary Market after a period of time. This can also be done for Bonds and other products.

Market Makers: These are simply Traders that stand by to buy or sell stocks, as the firm they are part of more than likely was involved in the issuance of the stock. These desks generally have a list of stocks that they will, at any given time, buy or sell to provide liquidity to the marketplace.

Emerging Markets: These are stocks of companies that are based in emerging countries or whose economies are not as strong as some of the bigger ones. Third World countries would fall in to this. Usually most Eastern European, some Asian and Latin American countries and companies are included in this group.

International: This is really a USA phenomenon. This desk will support Non-US stocks that are not part of the Emerging Markets portfolio. There are more developed countries and companies within such.

Options: There are many types of Options. In short, these provide clients the option to buy (Calls) or sell (Puts) stocks at certain prices, known as a strike price. Investors will pay premiums and be able to have exposure to more shares without having to purchase the shares at the price the actual stock is trading at. These are used for speculation and hedging positions. Investors are gambling that a stock will go up or down within a period of time. If a client owns a stock, for an example of hedging, they may buy a put to limit their downside exposure, as if the stock does drop, they have the option to sell that stock at an agreed level.

Fixed Income can be summarized by saying it is Bonds. Bonds are representation of credit, meaning organizations will issue Bond notes and they agree to pay the owner of the note interest (Coupon Rate) over a certain period of time until the Bond matures (Maturity Date), at which time the owner will receive back the principal of the note. The Fixed Income business, as mentioned, breaks down into two sub-groups, Credit and Rates, with further breakouts within each. These groups generally consist of:

Rates

US Government Bonds: The US Government issues paper to raise capital. They have many forms, some of which are Treasury Bills and Treasury Notes. Like all other Bonds, they pay interest and have maturity dates. US Government paper is considered very safe, as it is backed by the credit of the US Government.

Emerging Markets or Sovereign Bonds: Like the US, other countries will issue notes to raise capital as well, also backed by the credit and good faith of the respective governments.

Municipal Bonds: These are bonds that are issued by States and Municipalities to finance various projects such as road construction, electricity, schools, etc. These notes are backed by the credit of the county, state or municipality that is issuing them.

Money Markets: Also referred to as short term paper. These are products such as Commercial Paper and Certificates of Deposit that range in maturity from 1 day to 365 days. They will pay interest and principal at maturity.

Mortgage Backed Securities: There are many types of Mortgage Backed Securities (MBS). These are Bonds in which the underlying assets are mortgages that are pooled by maturity dates and then sold off in bond form. The more common types are Government National Mortgage Association (GNMA), Federal National Mortgage Association (FNMA) or Federal Home Loan Mortgage Association Corporation (FHLMC). A majority of the Mortgage Loans in the US goes through these organizations and they repackage them and sell them in the securities market.

Repurchase Agreements: Also known as REPO. This is a financing transaction, similar to swaps. There are Regular, Reverse and Tri Party Repurchase agreements. In these transactions, securities are lent out for fees with the understanding that the lender will purchase them back, hence the term Repurchase agreement. It is a basic way of financing trading inventory that normally would sit dormant and attract internal costs due to the use of funds that was allocated to purchase them to begin with. This product has grown over the years and almost all products are REPO'd these days.

Foreign Exchange: Known as FX. This is the buying and selling of the various currencies around the world.

Commodity Futures: Futures are options. They trade in contracts just like options do. This is widely done in the Commodities market with things like Copper, Gold, Cotton, Frozen Concentrated Orange Juice, Silver, etc., though it has expanded to almost anything. You can even buy wine futures today. Investors will speculate they are going up or down.

Credit

Corporate: These are bonds that Corporations have issued. They trade based upon the credit rating of the company that issues them. Where Commercial paper has maturity dates of less than a year, Corporate bonds will usually have maturities of at least a year past issuance date.

Distressed/High Yield: These are sometimes called "Junk bonds," as they are forms of Corporate bonds, but the issuing companies normally have a credit rating off BB or less.

International: Just like International Equities, these are bonds that International, non-US firms issue.

Each product line within Fixed Income will usually trade Derivatives of each as well. Derivatives are a very important yet complex mechanism to hedge inventory and play a vital role in every major trading strategy these days. Some types of derivatives within the Fixed Income world are:

Credit Default: These are swaps on credits. They price and trade based on the likelihood that a Creditor will default on its bond payments or has some other type of credit event like a restructuring or bankruptcy. The buyer pays a fixed cash flow and receives a payoff if there is a credit event.

Interest Rate: These are swaps based on the volatility of Interest rates. One side thinks rates will go up and the other thinks they will go down. Generally one side takes a fixed rate amount and the other a variable. There are different types of Interest rates as well; the most common in this product line is LIBOR (London Interbank Overnight Rate), what banks will charge for borrowing money overnight.

Foreign Exchange: These are swaps on currencies. An FX swap combines a spot transaction (spot value date is usually two business days to settle) and an opposite outright forward (future settlement date). These are very important instruments for risk management and cross-currency liquidity management as more and more firms generate revenue in more than one currency.

Total Return: These are swaps in which one counterparty receives the total return (interest payments and any gains or losses) from a specific asset and the other counterparty receives a negotiated cash flow that is not related to the credit value of the related asset. These are also known as Total Rate of Return Swaps.

Then there is the Prime Brokerage business which interacts with most of these products as well, but is more service-oriented. There can be a trade execution relationship for these clients if they wish to do so. Prime Brokerage at its most basic component is a business of selling Operational services. Many firms, usually of small to medium size, cannot absorb the expenses associated with supporting their trading activity, and as such choose to hire another firm to do so—outsourcing if you will. This is predominantly done from a clearing of trades' perspective, but it does involve much more. Firms will execute trades with other firms, then report those trades to the Prime Broker to settle them on their behalf. In some cases, the prime broker is also the executing broker of the trade. The Prime Broker will hold assets on the client's behalf and perform reporting on the assets and transactions, as well as provide financing capabilities for the client. Sometimes the client will not have the asset in the portfolio they traded and the Prime Broker will arrange to borrow those securities to make delivery. Prime Brokers make money by charging fees as well as obtaining spreads on the use of the client's assets, by either lending or financing the positions. Prime Brokerage is very heavy on Client Service, obviously, as this is the core of the business. Clients want timely communications and accurate reporting, in addition to broad financing at effective cost levels.

These are the main products and account structures within the main Business lines. There are others, and new products and account offerings are always in the works. The above covered the core components, though, as most all others are derivations of these or extensions of such.

MANAGING YOUR CAREER

One of my favorite parts of being an executive on Wall Street relates to educating and developing staff. No, I am not in Human Resources. I make time to talk with staff and I thoroughly enjoy it. I interviewed literally hundreds of folk that were about to or just did enter Wall Street, and I can say with no hesitation, not one of them truly knew what they wanted to do with their careers and subsequently their lives. This is not to say they were ignorant; quite the contrary. Some of them are very successful today and continue to climb the corporate ladder. They were uneducated and uninformed about Wall Street. This is not a negative thing. It is reality, and I am happy to inform you it is correctable. However, it will require your commitment to knowledge and it takes years of experience. You see, my view was that I was only as good as the people I was surrounded by. I didn't always have a choice of who they were. Many managers in any industry forget to share the knowledge and experiences they have and subsequently do not lead. They get engulfed in their own worlds and are blinded to this concept. I would say this is a narrow-minded view on yourself and your organization. You truly are only as good as the people you are surrounded by. It is an absolute requirement that time is made to educate them. Technology is a fabulous tool, but to me the most valuable commodity of any business is its people and, just like technology, it needs to be invested in. I was fortunate enough to travel the world and get involved with a wide array of Wall Street products and practices. I always felt the need to share that knowledge. It was instilled in me by my mentors, the pioneers of processing on Wall Street. I started on Wall Street at the bottom right after High School and worked my way up. I retained every experience and built on them as my career progressed. But enough about me—let's get on to you and the valuable topics we will need to cover. Something for you to keep in mind as we start this: your career is a journey, not a destination. One of the best managers I ever worked for told me that years ago and it has stuck with me.

Lesson 1—Knowledge is King!!

I am a huge buyer of knowledge. The more knowledge you have, the more valuable you are. The more valuable you are, the more opportunities will be presented. The more opportunities that are presented, the more chances you have to show what you are made of and if you deliver, you will be rewarded. Knowledge truly is the most valuable commodity that I know of.

In every development session I held, my opening line would be, "It is not who dies with the most toys that wins, it is who dies with the most knowledge." This couldn't be more true than on Wall Street: the more knowledge you have, the stronger you are.

Knowledge comes in many forms. It could be product, skill set, leadership, functions, procedures or many other things. The trick is to tie them all together. The most important is the knowledge of communications. I will get to that later.

So how do you get knowledge? I have found the best way to obtain knowledge is by doing what you wish to learn about. Want to learn basketball? Go find a court and start shooting. Want to learn about a job? Start doing the job. I was never one for reading to master something else. One of my mentors over the years told me at the beginning of my career that "if you do a job on Wall Street for more than a two year period with no derivation to it, you are wasting the firm's time." I have a slightly different twist on it. I say you are wasting your own time. It prompted me to develop the below.

The Boxes of Knowledge.

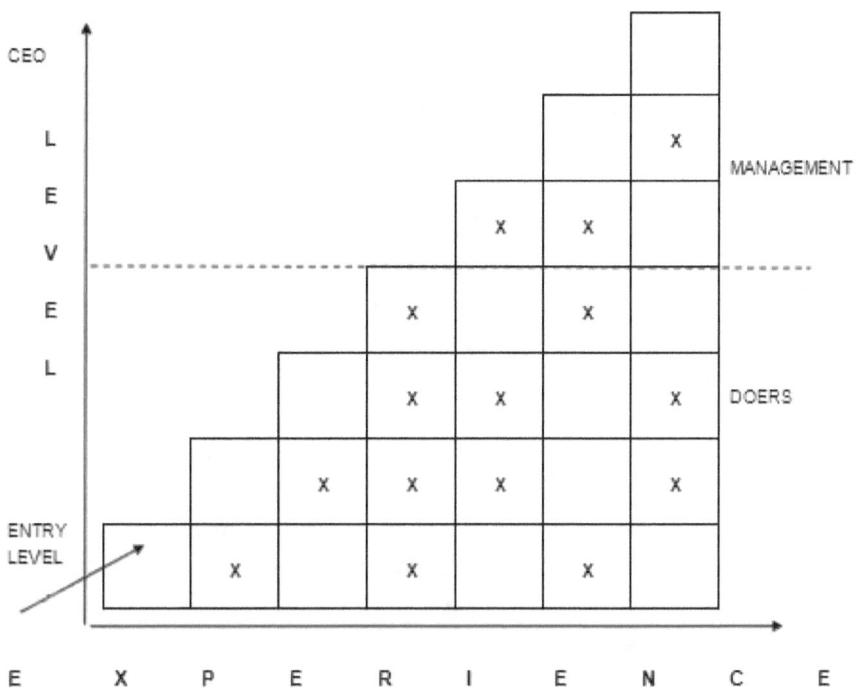

The above graph depicts your career. Most people get an entry level job, unless they are MBAs out of Harvard, etc., and start at the bottom without truly knowing what the job is they took and how it fits into the bigger picture of the firm and industry. The X axis represents your experience while the Y axis represents your growth up the corporate ladder. The trick is to fill in as many of the boxes as possible. You may get a job as a margin bookkeeper and that could lead to a clearance role and subsequently to supervising a small team. By doing this, you're expanding your knowledge. Each time you move on to a new role, you need to link up all the areas you have worked in and understand how they interact. Then enrich this with the process of seeking information on your own.

There is a dotted line through the middle. I would always ask people why I drew this. Not many got it right. It is there to represent different skill sets and a milestone in your career growth. Being a manager or leader and being what I call a doer (the ones who are processing the widgets) requires a completely different set of skills. The best doers arenot necessarily the best managers and the best managers are not necessarily the best doers.

However, I can assure you the manager that understands the details of the doers is much better off than one that doesn't. I feel sorry for any manager that doesn't know what they are managing. Managing and leading require that you understand the firm and its strategic goals and that you can communicate these goals to a wide array within the foodchain, manage budgets, develop people and still do your day job impeccably. The doers typically know what each day is going to bring. They have to process X number of widgets. The manager has to be flexible and versatile to deal with the daily fires in the organization as well as the lunatics above. Yes, everyone has a boss, regardless of their level. The line also represents what I believe to be the most difficult level in your career, the reason being that you clearly did well at processing to get there, but now you have a whole new pressure set to contend with. I call it the triple whammy. First, you still must maintain your level of being the best subject matterexpert of what you process. You now also have to learn how to manage and lead in addition to dealing with management above you—not an easy task to master, I assure you. Most people peak at this level as they remain in the subject matter expert stage and do not make the time to further educate themselves. Or even worse, the managers above them don't take the time to ensure they are trained and guided.

The most talented individuals I have met in my career understood all of this and used it to their advantage. It is about constantly growing. One mentor told me once, "you should learn something new every day or you wasted the day." He was right! Your career is a journey, not a destination. Never stop learning and trying to advance. This is one of the fundamental principles that the industry has been built on. I would ask people what are you learning these days and I would get responses back like, "I don't have time because I am so busy in my day." This is absolute garbage. Think about it this way. You will spend an average of 50 hours a week working. If you are saying that you cannot make at least one hour a week to learn something new, you are selling yourself short.

The other item is change. Change is inevitable. Don't be scared of it. Embrace it. Nurture it. Don't be overtaken by it. You want to ride that wave. When the wave stops, look for another one. I promise you there will be another one. I highly recommend you are the driving force of change. Hope is not a strategy and complacency is not an option.

Lesson 2—The only stupid question or idea is the one you don't ask or tell!!

If you do not ask, don't expect anyone to tell you. Wall Street is a massive puzzle and very few are knowledgeable enough to educate you on all of it. Even the ones that are don't necessarily have the time or inclination to share it. You will need to put the puzzle together. You are responsible for asking questions and for your own development. Learning is at a minimum 85% yourself and 15% your manager's responsibility. You are the one responsible for gaining knowledge and managing your career. Too many people on Wall Street work in a silo. What I mean by this is that everyone is focused on their little piece of the puzzle. The best and brightest I have met in my career get the big picture. They know the overall business and they understand how all the components on Wall Street fit together. The only way to gain some of this knowledge is by asking questions and putting the puzzle together. Different individuals will have some of the answers. You need to get in front of those people and ask questions and link the answers you receive from all. It is not easy, as sometimes people think they know what they are talking about and they really don't. Be savvy and recognize this and move on to the next person who can help you. But it is an absolute requirement for your education to ask questions, every day!!! Do not be embarrassed if you don't know something. Nobody knows everything and the ones that think they do, usually don't. I can recall in one of my development sessions with an employee I stated this lesson. She was horrified. I asked why and she told me she didn't know what and who to ask. I asked her what she wanted to know. She hadn't given it thought. I asked her to go away for a day or so and think about exactly what she wanted to gain knowledge about. She did and when she came back a day later she said she was interested in the Credit department. I asked her what she knew about that department. Needless to say, she knew practically nothing. I said that is your first question. What is the Credit department? What does the Credit department do? I proceeded to explain to her what that area of the firm did and it was like a light bulb went off. I couldn't stop her from asking more questions. The opening question can be basic. What do you do? What is this department about? Why is it needed? The important thing is to ask and never be scared. If someone says

"That's a stupid question" you know you are talking to wrong person and proceed to move on to the next person. Not knowing is not a crime. Not asking is.

I would prompt people to ask questions about the job and firm, even the industry. The thing is that once you ask one and the answers are provided, it sparks you to ask more as the answer is being provided. It is contagious, I promise. Just as important, it gets your creative juices flowing and ideas start being created. Even the craziest ideas might have an ounce of good in them. The other thing is that if people are generating the idea and they are let loose to run with it, they will feel ownership of it and the chances of it being delivered have just dramatically improved. So don't be shy. Step up and generate those ideas. Management always says they want to hear them and in today's environment, firms are always looking for ways to be leaner, more efficient and more productive.

Lesson 3—Be Persistent!!

Don't be scared to ask someone to sit and chat with you. I recall an article years ago in which a recent college graduate had a desire to work for one of the major firms and only that one. It was his dream. He sent his resume and heard nothing. Called multiple times. Nothing. He didn't give up. He was committed to working there and achieving his dream of being a Master of the Universe. So he went to the headquarters in lower Manhattan andwaited for the CEO to show up. Every day for weeks, he would just go and wait for a chance of seeing the CEO. Finally, one day he saw him and walked up and introduced himself. He apologized for bothering him but begged for a minute of his time. He proceeded to tell the CEO his dream. The CEO made the time to meet with him at a later date. The CEO was impressed with his persistence and offered him an entry level job. The story goes that the man went on to be one of the most successful traders in that firm's history.

Have a goal and don't be afraid to go after it. If someone is not willing to help you, keep knocking on doors until you find someone who is. Take time to educate yourself as well, but be completely dedicated to you and your success. These days the industry is getting colder and colder, and the old days of loyalty from the firm to the employee are gone. You have to be loyal to yourself and go out and make your opportunities. No one is going to create a path of success for you except you.

When doors of opportunity get opened, make the most of them. If you are seeking knowledge about a particular issue, do not rest on just one answer. On Wall Street, there are many answers to the same question. It is the creative nature of the beast. Be persistent in chasing answers and solutions. Never sit still.

There are three types of people on Wall Street: the sheep, the status quo and the rock stars. The sheep get slaughtered. Period. These days, there are very few sheep out there, if any. They have mostly been eliminated through the last 10 years or so. There are still a few. Some names come to mind immediately. Anyway, the latter two, status quo and rock star, are completely a personal decision that you only can make. For the record, there is nothing wrong with either one. Both are legitimate and honest ways to live. It is simply the decision to be the best or stay in a comfort zone and fly under the radar. At a minimum, 80% of the people on Wall Street are status quo. They come and do their jobs with very little variance. They are the 9 to 5ers: no more, no less. They do what is expected. There is nothing wrong with this. You can make a very nice career. But then again, do not expect opportunities to be thrown your way, nor should you expect to be compensated through the roof. Be happy with what you get. Wall Street still pays better than most industries. Now the rock star to me is the place you want to be. You are constantly looking to do things better, faster, more efficiently, cheaper, driving change and preserving revenue. These are the ones that wake up every single day and say, "I can make a difference." These are typically the ones that get ahead. They get the promotions, the glory and ultimately the fat paychecks. Again, it is a personal decision. Do you want to rock-n-roll or sit down? Think about it. I say let's Rock!!!

Lesson 4—Be Prepared!!

The people that can help you are very busy. If they are making the time to help you, don't waste their time by showing up unprepared. That is a surefire way to get shown the door. Think about what you would like to obtain from them and be considerate of their time.

As a matter of fact, whenever you have meetings, be prepared. Jot down some key points that you need answered or items you want to make sure are covered—nothing formal, just some bullet points. Bring it with you and take notes. I can't tell you how many times I referred back to my notes from a meeting. Once the meeting starts, try to keep it on track and going in the direction you need to ensure your questions are being answered.

Depending on who you are meeting with, you might want to practice and rehearse how you will be presenting. Some folks on Wall Street are very stiff and conservative. Others are laid back and approachable. Understand the audience you will be dealing with and be prepared to adjust to any style.

As I mentioned, I would hold regular skip levels with people in my organization. I was a pretty laid back and an approachable manager and as a result, some employees would come in thinking it would just be a convenient type of chat. I was most impressed when employees came in with their own agenda and knew exactly what they wanted to get out of the meeting with me. That is not to say that I didn't spend time with the others. I did, and I walked them through my agenda, not theirs.

The best one I ever experienced was an employee coming in with an actual list of questions. It was extremely well thought out and provided the entire framework for our discussion. I used the sheet as the focal point of the meeting and the employee was ensured I answered every question. She brought two copies as well, so she could follow along and make notes. It showed me the employee cared about her future as well as being considerate about my time.

Remember, you will usually be meeting with someone more senior than you. Wall Street is full of egos that like to be stroked. Play to that. Thank them for taking time out of their hectic day. Little comments like "It is refreshing someone at your level makes time to talk with the employees" or "Thank you for making the time to educate me", believe it or not, will get the meeting off to a good start and show the manager you are appreciative and serious about learning and advancing your knowledge and career. Make sure at the end you thank them as well. You would be amazed how many don't and it sticks in a manager's mind that the employee was unappreciative. If need be, ask if a follow up session can be held if you found it beneficial. Good managers will generally ask you if it was beneficial, but some don't. Leave nothing to chance, ever. Tell them if it was.

Lesson 5—Be Professional!!

I know it sounds obvious, but you would be amazed at how many folks take this for Granted, particularly when meeting with a laid back and outgoing manager. My dad used to say "just because someone else is jumping off the bridge doesn't mean you need to." The same concept applies here: Find your own groove and personality and stick to it in a professional manner. Wall Street loves the Corporate manner and has little tolerance for those that don't conform and toe the line. Leave all the immaturity at home with friends and family. The old saying "treat people like you want to be treated" is true, so be considerate.

When I was a child, I had a baseball coach that used to say if you dress like a ball player you will play like a ball player. It's true. Even in these days of casual attire, I wore a suit every day. Well, maybe not on a Friday unless I had a serious meeting. Look at every executive on Wall Street, or any other industry, for that matter. Almost all are wearing suits. Make sure you dress appropriately. The image you portray is very important to your success.

Be thoughtful in your communications. It shows you take this seriously and also shows you have respect for the manager. Whether you do or don't is irrelevant. Perception is reality in this industry and it can make or break careers. I have dealt with people that know nothing, but they display themselves professionally. One would like to believe that ultimately they will be found out, but you would be surprised how many folks have survived and thrived in this industry and really don't know what they are doing, but they portray themselves as if they do.

Wall Street is a tough and cold place, and there is no room for error. There is also no room for emotions. A mentor of mine said that once you show emotions, you're dead. It is like animals fighting: they smell blood, they know you are off balance and they go right for the jugular. There are loads of good and bad people on Wall Street and in life, as well. Act the same to all, whether you enjoy dealing with them or not. It makes no difference. My older brother called this the even-keeled model. He is a master of it. He never showed emotions and always treated everyone the same. If you don't like dealing with someone, try to avoid them. But I guarantee you can't avoid them all the time.

Be prompt also. Nothing irked me more than when someone asked my assistant to set up some time to chat with me and they showed up late. What is even worse, is not showing up at all. Make sure you get the meeting in the person's calendar and confirm it. Then get there on time. Be considerate of their time as well, so try not to over-extend your visit. Most managers will politely end the meeting when they need to. Usually one hour will suffice. They will tell you if it is too little or too much. You can always have follow-up sessions. If something comes up, make sure you have the meeting cancelled and apologize, regardless of the reason. It is considerate and appreciated.

Lesson 6—Deliver Results and Be a Partner!!

I had a senior manger once tell me that it isn't about results. I couldn't disagree more. It is always about delivering results. What he should have said is the results themselves are not the only thing. It is also very important how you go about delivering those results. The most important things in this industry are the production of revenue, the preservation of revenue and reduction of expenses. After all, it is the Financial industry. How you go about delivering these things is critical to your and the firm's success. In my book, servicing the client is right up on top, as well.

Someone who gets the job done but tramples over everyone to do it will not survive. They will not be respected and will be ostracized. The person that is inclusive and sensitive to needs of others while executing will thrive. Show boating and being a self-centered contributor is a losing plan.

Every day you should be thinking about the clients and your partners, whether you are producing revenue, preserving it or providing service to a client. Your primary thought should be delivering and executing on whatever it is you need to in an effort to be the leader in the market. To do this you must understand needs and desires of clients and partners. The only way to get that understanding is to discuss it openly and professionally. Once that understanding is there, a plan can be drafted, re-discussed and then executed.

Results are the center of it all: your development, your service, your accomplishments, revenue production and preservation and expense reduction. Never forget this. Be a team player and always keep the lines of communication open with your partners and clients. But remember to be sensitive and cognizant of the side they are coming from and gear the communications to that. In delivering results, you are second. The client and firm are first and foremost.

Just like any team, you cannot do it on your own. The team has to work together. When I worked in London, I worked very long hours. But even at the end of the day I would look around at my coworkers and ask if anyone needed help. I wanted to go home, but I didn't think it was fair for anyone else to stay. That is team work. We should all go home, I thought. Individual actions are seen but are not central to production. How the firm produces as a whole is most important. I am sure almost everyone has heard about bonuses on Wall Street, especially these days. Don't believe everything you hear. Yes I too believe bonuses at the highest levels are over-inflated. I mean, making $75 million in one year is a little over the top in any industry, in my opinion. An individual's bonus is or should be derived from three basic things: how well the firm did, how well the individual performed versus their peers and the fair market value of the role the employee is performing to the market. Most firms work off the first two but lose sight of the third.

In today's Wall Street, the reliance on others and partnership is even more important. So many areas are integrated. Functions are outsourced to other states or even countries. This is a trend that will continue even more. Strong relations and partnerships are essential.

In today's technological world, too many folks rely on email or instant messaging. These are useful tools, but I promise you they can never replace a good, old-fashioned phone call or face to face meeting. In fact, I can't tell you how many errors and losses I have seen because people don't pick up a phone. They said things like, "But I sent an email." Well guess what? Not everyone looks at emails in a timely manner. In a marketplace that is based on money, time is critical. Do not take technological advancements for granted and assume your IM or email was received. It might not have been. Pick up the phone, please. It works!

Lesson 7—Be Happy and Love what you Do!!

This is my favorite one, and I am adamant about it. You will spend at minimum 60% of your conscious work week doing the job—possibly more, depending on your role. If you are not enjoying yourself and having fun, the chances of you being successful are slim to none. The premise that you are what you do for a living is true. In many cases, as sad as it is, your job does define you. I highly recommend you don't let it. I would tell people your job is a means of allowing you to do other things, like having a house, taking vacations, paying for college, etc. Family and health come way before your job. Many people think the job is everything. Think of it this way: you can always get another job to make money, but you cannot always find another family and definitely cannot replace your health. Most people in this world do, unfortunately, have to work. I always believed the simple and most basic concepts work. No need to over complicate things. I always try to make the environment in the office a fun and easy-going one. My thought process is that if people are enjoying themselves, having fun and feel relaxed they will do a better job. It is logical and it works. If you like to do something, you will enjoy it and subsequently perform it better. On the other hand, if you don't like doing something and have to, chances are you will just go through the motions and won't do a very good job.

This concept is one of the fundamental reasons I have written this book. If people know what they are getting into and can obtain an understanding of the jobs and roles on Wall Street, it will aid them in making an educated decision of what field in the industry to get involved in based on personal desires.

You must love what you do and commit to it. This holds true in anything in life, really. The great thing about life is once you do not love something anymore, you can always find something else. Look at the divorce rate in the world today. Look at how many times people change jobs or even careers. No matter what you choose and no matter how many times you change, though, this concept applies. I am a firm believer in putting your heart into everything you do, and the work place is no exception.

To find something you love and enjoy doing, it must suit your personality and strengths. It must provide growth and challenge for you. It must provide you the opportunity to work on your weaknesses, and it should give you a path of education as well. I advise people to take an inventory of themselves. Sit down with a piece of paper and on one side list all the things you enjoy doing and on the other side what you do not. Try and be specific. Things like, I like going to the movies is not going to help on this one, but things like dealing with people, analyzing things, solving problems, flowing out or visualizing things. You can then refer to what I have outlined in *The Basics* chapter and align yourself with a career path. Good luck and always have fun. Enjoy and love whatever you choose to do in life.

Lesson 8—Observation is a Great Way to Learn!!

Ok, so I told you already that doing things is a great way to learn. Another excellent way that most people overlook is observing. On Wall Street this is actually required. Watching how people react in meetings or during good or bad times in the market is one of the best ways you can develop your behavior. I would go into meetings and sometimes not say a word—a rarity for me, by the way—and just observe people: how they sat, how they reacted to phrases, the emotions they were displaying, and listen to what they were saying and how. Wall Street is a stressful place, and how you react in that environment is critical to your success. By watching and observing individuals and how they carry themselves in certain situations, you can learn how to better handle yourself in different scenarios. For example, if you are sitting in a room with another employee, and you have your arms folded across your chest, this is an indication that you are closed to the conversation and not open for discussion. Body language is a very powerful form of communication and definitely provides insight to a person's thought process or perspective. The more senior you get, the more important this becomes. A mentor of mine called it executive presence. When certain people would walk into a room, you just knew the meeting was going to be taken control of. I mentioned previously that there is no room for emotions on Wall Street. Certain people carry themselves in a very confident and assuring manner. By watching examples of good and bad behavior, you can learn how to better handle yourself, depending on the situation you find yourself in.

Lesson 9—Metrics, Metrics, Metrics!!

Measuring yourself, your progress and your career is very important. Imagine a baseball game with no score. How would you know who wins? The same holds true for your career, performance and functions that you perform in your job. Metrics on Wall Street have become more and more important over the years. Six Sigma took this to all new levels. I would ask people how they know they were doing a good job. I would get answers back like "I just know" or "The business told me I am." Well, it's nice to know it or be told it by a partner, but at the end of the year when you go into your boss's office to discuss your performance and bonus, factual data will speak loads. It is one thing to say you will do something and do it; it is another to say you will do it and show it. One of my bosses once said to me that you cannot manage something unless you can measure it. He was right. Setting goals in your career and performance is important. You should do this and be realistic in setting those goals, but when you set them, be able to track your progress at any given point. Metrics and tracking issues, projects and exposure are even more important as you climb the corporate ladder. The more you are responsible for, the more difficult it is to keep track of. You will need to have metrics to manage what you are responsible over—at minimum, to maintain control and manage exposure, but also to identify trends and where to allocate staff. Another mentor taught me that measuring something for the sake of measuring it is absolutely worthless. Metrics must be meaningful. As an example, tracking trading volumes is somewhat useless, unless you are doing it for a reason such as you are being charged a certain amount per trade. Meaningful metrics tells a story. It displays progress or lack thereof. Showing trade volumes increasing while staff has decreased is a great story. You were able to handle more volume with less people. Always make sure there is a purpose to what you are measuring. Many mangers will ask for metrics for no true purpose. It is okay to ask and generate the ideas to make that metrics more useful. The same holds true for performance metrics. In certain parts of the industry, they have taken this to unbelievable extremes. A person's performance rating can be based solely on metrics. I am not a supporter of this, though, as performance is not always just about how many widgets you processed. This is still a people business and taking the personal side out of performance metrics is just wrong in my view. In performance reviews I held, I would have five goals for people, once above a certain level, of course. Four were generic and one specific to the individual's daily responsibilities or area. My view is that the four generic were important in any role that an individual was in and would make the person a stronger and better performer in the long run. These generic goals were Communications, Control, Technology and Efficiency. Communications was developing and maintaining relationships. Technology was partnering with technology to ensure proper tools and enhancements were being delivered. Control was running a controlled process or business function, while mitigating risk to the firm and/or organization. Efficiency was constantly improving things and making the process or functions better. I would then ask all to show me via metrics how they did it. These four things would stay with people their entire careers and were transferable to any role they might encounter as they continued their journey. Most important, they are measurable.

Lesson 10—You are Your Most Valuable Asset!!

I mentioned that you must make things happen for yourself. But it is absolutely critical that you possess the confidence in yourself to truly succeed. It is like the old saying, "you must love yourself before you can love others." Well, the same holds true for your career. If you do not believe in yourself and have the confidence to succeed, you will not and therefore will be of no benefit to an organization. Take stock in yourself. This is not to say you should be cocky or arrogant. This definitely does not work, and I have seen careers destroyed for those that acted that way. This is simply stating that you need to be confident in your abilities and display it in your actions—the walk softly and carry a big stick kind of thing. If you exude confidence the right way, it is seen and this will prompt others to have faith in you as well. All the knowledge and the skills you learn are useless without you realizing that you are the one that ultimately controls your destiny. There are choices to make in your life and career, and no one can make them but you. You must believe and know in your heart and soul that you are good. Doubt in yourself or your abilities is seen by others and acted upon, whether you realize it or not. Nobody can make you good but you, so stand up for yourself and take control of your destiny. Utilize the previous lessons to assist you in doing so, but again, be careful how you portray yourself to others. Remember, perception in many cases is reality!!

FINALLY!

My aspirations for you are simple: find something you love and enjoy doing, then excel at it. If this book has been able to assist anyone in achieving this, than I have achieved my goal of sharing my knowledge, experience and advice. May you always be blessed with love and may all of the wonderful gifts life has to offer be obtained throughout your long and pleasant journey of existence!!

Best of Luck.

ABOUT THE AUTHOR

Bob Alexander graduated from Boston University in 1990, having obtained a Bachelor of Science in Business Administration. He had his first job on Wall Street as a delivery messenger in the summer of 1984 with Salomon Brothers, after graduating High School. He subsequently worked on and off throughout his college years, holding various clerical jobs in Retail, Investment Management and Capital Markets with firms such as Mass Financial Services and Shearson Lehman Brothers. In 1990, Bob left Boston and returned to New York, where he obtained a role with one of the largest Investment Firms on Wall Street, Merrill Lynch. He spent over 18 years there developing his Management and Leadership skills. He started as a bookkeeper in International retail, performing standard books and records controls, and moved up to supervising Bank activity and controls. In 1994 he moved to London, England, where he managed Operational Control teams, Settlement areas and various projects. He moved back to New York in June 1996 to manage the Bank Loan trade support group, including Emerging Market products, Distressed assets and Lending businesses, and built a global infrastructure for the business by creating centers in London, Tokyo and Hong Kong. In 1998, he was requested to move to Hong Kong to be head of Fixed Income Operations for Southeast Asia. In 1999, he added to his responsibilities by taking on the operational Control team for the region. He moved back to the US in August 2000, having accepted a role within the Investment Management division located in Princeton, New Jersey. He managed various areas including Separate Account Management, 529 plans and Third party distribution. In 2002, he returned to Capital Markets running US Fixed Income Sales support within the Finance organization.

Within two years he had created such efficiencies that the role grew to become global for both Equity and Fixed Income. In early 2004, he accepted additional responsibilities over Capital Markets Client Data, building the Anti-Money Laundering facilities and expanding the Client Data group globally. He left that role in 2005 and became involved with multiple projects such as building a Global Brokerage Fee utility and reengineering Merrill's Structured Note issuance facility. He then assumed responsibility of Merrill's US Fixed Income Middle Office and Global Treasury Operations. In early 2007, he relinquished that role to run Client and Product Data as well as US Equity Middle Office and Prime Brokerage Operations. He accepted early retirement from the firm in November 2008 and started his own financing company, Alexander Financial Solutions. He is currently a Managing Director in Global Operations at Cantor Fitzgerald.

www.ingramcontent.com/pod-product-compliance
Lightning Source LLC
Chambersburg PA
CBHW021912170526
45157CB00005B/2050